FORGIVING
AND
FORGETTING

Dear Reader,

Here is a copy of the minibook you requested.

As the title suggests, it covers a subject rarely encouraged these days. Ours is a fight-back, get-even society where even the slightest offense often leads to a lawsuit. Hardly a week passes without my becoming aware of an offense someone is unwilling to let go of. What a drain on one's emotional tank . . . what a tragic way to live!

The book you hold in your hand offers the alternative: to forgive and forget. As you read it, I hope you will realize the devastating toll that revenge and bitterness can take on anyone who refuses to handle conflict God's way. And, with that realization, my prayer is that you will commit yourself to a life of forgiving and forgetting. There's really not a better way to live.

Chuck

CHARLES R. SWINDOLL

FORGIVING
AND
FORGETTING

INSIGHT FOR LIVING

This minibook is a revised and updated version of chapters 4 and 5 from *Improving Your Serve* (Waco, Tex.: Word Books, 1981). Used by permission.

Unless otherwise identified, all Scripture references are from the New American Standard Bible, © The Lockman Foundation 1960, 1962, 1963, 1968, 1971, 1972, 1973, 1975, 1977. Used by permission.

Printed in the United States of America.

COVER DESIGN: Steven Mitchell

INTRODUCTION

Most people have someone they could blame for something. Rip-offs and mistreatment abound; the list is endless:

- *A debt remains unpaid.*
- *A parent or boss or coach was unfair.*
- *Prejudice or partiality brought pain.*
- *A board member made life miserable.*
- *The jury declared the innocent guilty.*
- *Fraudulent investors took the money and ran.*
- *A mate was unfaithful.*
- *A partner lacking integrity failed to live up to his or her agreement.*
- *The physician made an incorrect diagnosis.*
- *The other guy got the credit for work you had done.*
- *A neighbor refuses to treat you fairly.*
- *Someone started a rumor that damaged your reputation.*
- *A pastor, whom you trusted and helped, used you.*
- *A friend turned on you.*
- *One of your children, now grown, won't speak to you.*

This minibook could literally be filled with stories I have heard and experiences I have had with people who were unfair, unfaithful, deceitful, or irresponsible. It would easily become a full-sized book if I included all the ramifications that grew out of each account. Virtually everywhere I travel I meet folks who have someone's face on their mental dart board. It is impossible to measure the amount of energy that is exerted every day through blame, resentment, and bitterness.

Rather than write about the obvious and more acceptable side of the problem, I have chosen to address the part that is seldom mentioned . . . and rarely applied. Admittedly, there are occasions when pressing for one's rights and retaliating for wrongs are correct actions. Crimes should be punished to the full extent of the law. Physical and sexual abuse should neither be excused nor tolerated. But more often than not, the negative thoughts that we cling to and blame others for do not fall into the category of criminal acts but rather personal offenses. Because we do not deal with them God's way, we continue to eat our heart out over things that aren't worth the energy drain.

And what is God's way? Forgiving and forgetting. As I heard recently, forgiveness is setting the prisoner free from bondage, only to discover that the prisoner was you!

My hope is that you will do three things with the pages that follow:

1. Read each page slowly and carefully. Don't hurry.

2. Take the message personally. Put yourself into the picture.
3. Apply it diligently. Even though it may seem too difficult to carry out, dare the risk.

Chuck Swindoll

Forgiveness is
the fragrance the
violet sheds on
the heel that has
crushed it.
　　—Mark Twain

FORGIVING

orgiveness is not an elective in the curriculum of life. It is a required course, and the exams are always tough to pass.

Several years ago I traveled to Trinity Evangelical Divinity School, a seminary located north of Chicago, in search of a pastoral intern. In the process of interviewing a number of men, I met a seminarian I will never forget. As it turned out, I did not select him to come as an intern, but I was extremely impressed with his sensitivity to God. Although young and inexperienced, his spirit was tender and he spoke with gentleness. It was obvious that the Lord was deeply at work in his life. The marks of a servant's heart were clearly visible—so much so, I probed to discover why. Among other things, he related an incredible true story that illustrated how God was molding him and shaping him through one of those tough "forgiveness exams." As best as I can remember, here's his story. I'll call him Aaron, not his real name.

Late one spring he was praying about having a significant ministry the following summer. He asked God for a position to open up on some church staff or in a Christian organization. Nothing happened. Summer arrived, still nothing. Days were turning into weeks, and Aaron finally faced reality—he needed *any* job he could find. He checked the want ads and the only thing that seemed a possibility was driving a bus on the south side of

9

Chicago . . . nothing to brag about, but it would help with tuition in the fall. After learning the route, he was on his own—a rookie driver in a dangerous section of the Windy City. It wasn't long before Aaron realized just *how* dangerous his job really was.

A small gang of tough kids spotted the young driver and began to take advantage of him. For several mornings in a row they got on, walked right past him without paying, ignored his warnings, and rode until they decided to get off . . . all the while making sarcastic remarks to him and others on the bus. Finally, he decided this had gone on long enough.

The next morning, after the gang got on as usual, Aaron saw a policeman on the next corner, so he pulled over, invited the officer aboard, and reported the offense. The cop told them to pay or get off. They paid . . . but unfortunately the policeman got off. And *they* stayed on. When the bus turned another corner or two, the gang assaulted the young driver.

When he came to, blood was all over his shirt, two teeth were missing, both eyes were swollen, his money was gone, and the bus was empty. After returning to the terminal and being given the weekend off, our friend went to his little apartment, sank onto his bed, and stared at the ceiling in disbelief. Resentful thoughts swarmed his mind. Confusion, anger, and disillusionment added fuel to the fire of his physical pain. He spent a fitful night wrestling with his Lord.

How can this be? Where's God in all of this? I genuinely want to serve Him. I prayed for a ministry. I was willing to serve Him anywhere, doing anything . . . and this is the thanks I get!

On Monday morning Aaron decided to press charges. With the help of the officer who had encountered the gang and several who were willing to testify as witnesses against the thugs, most of them were rounded up and taken to the local county jail. Within a few days there was a hearing before the judge.

In walked Aaron and his attorney plus the angry gang members, who glared across the room in his direction. Suddenly, Aaron was seized with a whole new series of thoughts. Not bitter ones, but compassionate ones! As a Christian, his heart went out to the guys who had attacked him. Under the Spirit's control he no longer hated them—he pitied them. They needed help, not more hate. What could he do? Or say? For sure, blame wasn't the answer.

Suddenly, after there had been a plea of guilty, Aaron—to the surprise of his attorney and everybody else in the courtroom—stood to his feet and requested permission to speak.

Your Honor, I would like you to total up all the days of punishment against these young men—all the time sentenced against them—and I request that you allow me to go to jail in their place.

The judge was absolutely dumbfounded. Both attorneys were stunned. As Aaron looked over at the gang members, whose mouths and eyes looked like saucers, he smiled and said quietly, "It's because I forgive you."

Once the judge reached a level of composure, he said rather firmly: "Young man, you're out of order. This sort of thing has never been done before!" To which the young man replied with genius insight:

> *Oh, yes, it has, Your Honor . . . yes, it has. It happened over nineteen centuries ago when a man from Galilee paid the penalty that all mankind deserved. In fact, He took the punishment on their behalf.*

And then, for the next three or four minutes, without interruption, he explained how Jesus Christ died for sinful humanity, thereby proving God's love and forgiveness.

He was not granted his request, but the young seminarian visited the gang members in jail, led most of them to faith in Christ, and began a significant ministry to many behind bars as well as to others on the south side of Chicago.

He passed a tough exam. And, as a result, a large door of ministry—the very thing he'd prayed for—opened up before him. Through the pain of extreme mistreatment, Aaron began to get a handle on what it means to forgive.

GOD'S FORGIVENESS OF US

As we undertake a subject this broad, it's necessary that we focus most of our thoughts on horizontal forgiveness rather than vertical forgiveness. But instead of ignoring the vertical altogether, perhaps I should briefly explain its significance. Actually, it's God's forgiveness of us that makes possible our forgiving others.

When the penalty of our sin was paid in full by Jesus Christ on the cross, God's wrath was expressed against Him—the One who took our place. God was therefore satisfied in that epochal sacrifice . . . allowing all who would turn, in faith, to the Son of God to be totally, permanently, and once-for-all forgiven. Christ's blood washed away our sin. And from the moment we believe on Him, we stand forgiven, relieved of guilt before a satisfied God, freeing Him to shower upon us His grace and love.

Remember the verse from that grand old song the church has sung for years?

> My sin—O, the bliss of this glorious thought,
> My sin . . . not in part but the whole,
> Is nailed to the cross and I bear it no more,
> Praise the Lord, praise the Lord, O my soul![1]

That says it well, but not as beautifully

as the song from the oldest of all hymnals—
the Psalms:

> Bless the Lord, O my soul;
> And all that is within me, bless His
>   holy name.
> Bless the Lord, O my soul,
> And forget none of His benefits;
> Who pardons all your iniquities;
> Who heals all your diseases;
> Who redeems your life from the pit;
> Who crowns you with lovingkindness
>   and compassion;
> Who satisfies your years with good
>   things,
> So that your youth is renewed like the
>   eagle. . . .
> He has not dealt with us according to
>   our sins,
> Nor rewarded us according to our
>   iniquities.
> For high as the heavens are above the
>   earth,
> So great is His lovingkindness toward
>   those who fear Him.
> As far as the east is from the west,
> So far has He removed our transgres-
>   sions from us.
> (Ps. 103:1–5, 10–12)

That's what Aaron helped those Chicago
thugs to understand. Through his model, they
had little difficulty realizing what Christ ac-
complished on the cross on their behalf. But

what they did not understand at the time was that Aaron could never have done that for them, horizontally, if it had not been for what Christ had already done for Aaron, vertically. Not until we fully accept and *appropriate* God's infinite and complete forgiveness on our behalf can we carry out the things I write about on the remaining pages. I think Martyn Lloyd-Jones summed this up well:

> *Whenever I see myself before God and realize something of what my blessed Lord has done for me at Calvary, I am ready to forgive anybody anything. I cannot withhold it. I do not even want to withhold it.*

OUR FORGIVENESS OF ONE ANOTHER

It doesn't take long before anyone who gets serious about walking closely with the living Lord must come to terms with forgiving others. Yes, *must*. As I said earlier, it's a required course in life's curriculum. Since this is such a common occurrence, I find it helpful to break the subject down into manageable parts, with handles I can get hold of.

Only Two Possibilities

When a wrong has been done against another person, there are only two possibilities. Either we have done it against another or it has been done against us. But whether we are responsible for the offense or the recipients of it, the first move is always ours. A Christian refuses to keep score. The general principle is set forth in Ephesians 4:31–32, which says:

> *Let all bitterness and wrath and anger and clamor and slander be put away from you, along with all malice. And be kind to one another, tender-hearted, forgiving each other, just as God in Christ also has forgiven you.*

That's a beautiful summation of the whole subject of forgiveness. It describes how to live with a clear conscience and thus be free to serve others as God's representative on earth. And observe the reminder—you forgive others (horizontal) "as God in Christ also has forgiven you" (vertical). But we need to get more specific. Let's analyze both sides of the forgiveness coin.

When You Are the Offender

Matthew 5:23–24 describes the correct response and procedure to follow when we have been in the wrong and offended someone. Read the two verses very carefully.

> *"If therefore you are presenting your offering at the altar, and there remember that your brother has something against you, leave your offering there before the altar, and go your way; first be reconciled to your brother, and then come and present your offering."*

The scene is clear. A person in Jesus' day has come to worship. At that time, in keeping with the Jewish law and custom, worshipers brought sacrificial animals or birds with them. The sacrifice would be slain before God, providing cleansing of sin and a way of open access to prayer. Today it would simply be a Christian's coming to the heavenly Father in prayer. Either way, while in prayer the worshiper is suddenly seized with an inescapable thought—the painful realization that he or she has offended another person. In the words of Jesus, you "remember that your brother has something against you." What do you do?

Stop! Don't ignore that realization. Don't just plunge on into prayer, even though that may be your first inclination. God wants us, rather, to be sensitive to His quiet prompting.

In verse 24 we are instructed to do four things:

Stop	"leave your offering there"
Go	"go your way"
Reconcile	"first be reconciled"
Return	"then come and present your offering"

The key term is *reconciled.* It's from a Greek root verb that means "to alter, to change" . . . with a prefix attached to the verb that means "through." In other words, we are commanded to go through a process that will result in a change. Clearly, the offender is to initiate the action.

One reliable authority defines *reconciled* rather vividly: "To change enmity for friendship . . . mutual concession after mutual hostility."[2] And another: "Seeing to it that the angry brother . . . renounces his enmity."[3]

That needs little clarification. We are to go (ideally, personally—if not possible, at least by phone or letter) and confess both the wrong and our grief over the offense, seeking the forgiveness of the one we wounded. *Then,* we are free to return to God in worship and prayer. Our goal is to "be reconciled."

But what if he or she won't forgive? Good question! The important thing for each of us to remember is that you are responsible for *you* and I am responsible for *me.* With the right motive, in the right spirit, at the right time, out of obedience to God, we are to humble ourselves and attempt to make things right. God will honor our efforts. The one offended may need time—first to get over the shock, and next to have God bring about a change in his or her heart. Healing sometimes takes time. Occasionally, a lot of time. I know of situations where it took months!

What if the situation only gets worse? Another good question frequently asked. This can happen. You see, during your silence, the one offended has been blaming you . . . mentally sticking pins in your doll . . . thinking all kinds of bad things about you. When you go to make things right, you suddenly cause the person's internal scales to go haywire. You remove any reason to blame, leaving only the person's guilt—which does a number on him or her, resulting in even worse feelings. But now it's no longer your fault. Illustration? King Saul and young David. In case you don't remember, David became a threat to the paranoid monarch. No matter how hard he tried to win back the favor of Saul, things only got worse. It took *years* for the troubled king to realize that David was sincere in his efforts to make things right. Again, it may take awhile for God to get through. My suggestion to you? Patiently wait and pray.

What if I decide to simply deal with it before God and not go through the hassle and embarrassment of talking with the other person? (We'll do *anything* to make things easier, won't we?) Well, first off, that is a willful contradiction of the command. Jesus says, "Stop, go, reconcile, and return!" *Not* to go is direct disobedience. It also can result in things getting worse.

Let's say I am driving away from your church parking lot next Sunday morning. I back my car into the side of your beautiful, new Mercedes 450 SEL. CRUNCH! You are visiting with friends following the service and you hear the noise. Your stomach churns as you see me get out of the car, look at the damage on yours . . . and then quietly bow in prayer:

Dear Lord, please forgive me for

*being so preoccupied and clumsy. And
please give John grace as he sees the
extensive damage I have caused out of
sheer negligence. And provide his needs
as he takes this car to have it fixed.
Thanks, Lord. Amen.*

As I drive away, I wave and smile real big
as I yell out the window, "It's all cleared up,
John. I claimed the damage before God. *Isn't
grace wonderful!*"

Tell me, how would that grab you? I have
rather strong doubts that it would suddenly
make things A-OK, no matter how sincere my
prayer might have been. You and I know it
would do no good. Prayer was never intended
to be a substitute for one's own responsibility.

When I was a kid we used to sing a little
chorus in church that sounded so pious, so
right. In fact, we would often close our youth
meetings by holding hands in a circle and sing-
ing this piece with our eyes closed:

*If I have wounded any soul today,
If I have caused one foot to go astray,
If I have walked in my own wilful
        way—
Good Lord, forgive!*[4]

I now question the message of that nice-
sounding song. Wounded souls are offended
people. And the Savior does not say, "Simply
pray and I'll forgive you." In fact, He says,
"Stop praying until you have made things

right!" This is the part of the "forgiveness exam" that's tough to pass.

One final question before moving on to the other side of the coin: What if it is impossible for me to reconcile because the offended person has died? Obviously, you cannot contact the dead. It's impossible to get a hearing, but your conscience still badgers you. In unique cases like these, I recommend that you share your burden of guilt with someone you can trust. A close friend, your mate, a counselor, or your pastor. Be specific and completely candid. Pray with that individual and confess openly the wrong and the guilt of your soul. In such cases—and only in such cases—prayer and the presence of an understanding, affirming individual will provide the relief you need so desperately.

After David had indirectly murdered Uriah, Bathsheba's husband, his guilt was enormous. Adultery and hypocrisy on top of murder just about did him in. If you want to know the depth of his misery, try to imagine the misery he confesses in Psalm 32:3–4:

> When I kept silent about my sin, my
>   body wasted away
> Through my groaning all day long.
> For day and night Thy hand was heavy
>   upon me;
> My vitality was drained away as with
>   the fever heat of summer.

Finally, when it all caved in on top of

David—when he broke the hypocritical silence and sought God's forgiveness—Uriah was not there to hear his confession. He had been dead the better part of a year. But David was not alone. A prophet named Nathan was there, the one who had confronted David with his sin. When the broken king poured out his soul, "I have sinned . . . ," Nathan followed quickly with these affirming words: "The Lord also has taken away your sin; you shall not die" (2 Sam. 12:13).

When you have been the cause of an offense—that is, when you are the offender—ask the Lord to give you the heart of a humble servant. Stop, go, reconcile, and then return. Trust me, you will never regret making things right. Never.

When You Are the Offended

Consider next Matthew 18:21–35 . . . same book, same Teacher, similar subject, but a different style and setting entirely from the Matthew 5 passage where Jesus delivered a monologue communicating a large number of things to His disciples. He touched on each rather generally, all great truths . . . but many subjects. However, in chapter 18 He is engaged in more of a dialogue, dealing in depth with the right response toward someone who offends us. Rather than dump the whole truckload on you, let me present these verses in sections.

First, the disciple's question:

Then Peter came and said to Him, "Lord, how often shall my brother sin against me and I forgive him? Up to seven times?" (Matt. 18:21)

Good, relevant question. What's the limit we should place on forgiveness? Peter was feeling magnanimous that day, for the going rate (according to the rabbis) was three times. The Jews were instructed to forgive once, forgive twice . . . and a third time, but from then on, forget it! Peter doubled the limit, then added a bonus for good measure. Not bad for a former fisherman who was never known for being a wimp!

Now, the Lord's response:

"I do not say to you, up to seven times, but up to seventy times seven." (v. 22)

Obviously, He is not saying literally, "Would you believe 490, Peter?" No, not that. He's suggesting an *infinite* number of times. *Limitless.* I would imagine that thought blew those disciples away . . . for sure, Peter! Which, no doubt, prompted Jesus to go into greater detail. Hence, a parable with a punch line. Read the story very carefully, preferably aloud and slowly.

"For this reason the kingdom of heaven may be compared to a certain king who wished to settle accounts with his slaves. And when he had begun to settle them,

there was brought to him one who owed
him ten thousand talents. But since he
did not have the means to repay, his
lord commanded him to be sold, along
with his wife and children and all that
he had, and repayment to be made.
The slave therefore falling down, pros-
trated himself before him, saying, 'Have
patience with me, and I will repay you
everything.' And the lord of that slave
felt compassion and released him and
forgave him the debt. But that slave
went out and found one of his fellow
slaves who owed him a hundred de-
narii; and he seized him and began to
choke him, saying, 'Pay back what you
owe.' So his fellow slave fell down and
began to entreat him, saying, 'Have
patience with me and I will repay you.'
He was unwilling however, but went
and threw him in prison until he should
pay back what was owed. So when his
fellow slaves saw what had happened,
they were deeply grieved and came and
reported to their lord all that had happened. Then summoning him, his lord
said to him, 'You wicked slave, I forgave you all that debt because you en-
treated me. Should you not also have
had mercy on your fellow slave, even
as I had mercy on you?' And his lord,
moved with anger, handed him over to
the torturers until he should repay all

that was owed him." (vv. 23–34)

By now I hope you have begun to think in terms of vertical forgiveness and horizontal forgiveness. The vertical is clearly seen in the first part of Jesus' parable. The man owed an incredible debt (about ten million dollars!) requiring infinite forgiveness, which the king provided—a beautiful reminder of God's forgiving the sinner.

The horizontal comes in view in the latter part of the story. That same slave, having just been forgiven his incredibly large debt, turned against one who owed him *less than twenty bucks* and assaulted the poor fellow. When the king got word of his violent reaction, he was furious. I mean, he was beside himself! And the confrontation that followed was understandably severe.

A couple of principles emerge from the latter part of this story that provide us with reasons to forgive others.

First: To refuse to forgive is hypocritical. Note again verses 32–33.

> *"Then summoning him, his lord said to him, 'You wicked slave, I forgave you all that debt because you entreated me. Should you not also have had mercy on your fellow slave, even as I had mercy on you?'"*

Since we have been the recipients of maximum mercy from God, who had every

25

right and reason to condemn us, then who are we to demand immediate and total justice from others? The compassion God (who is illustrated in the parable as the king) demonstrates on our behalf calls for us to do the same toward others. Anything less is nothing short of hypocritical.

Second: To refuse to forgive inflicts inner torment upon us. Remember how the story ends? It is exceedingly significant. "And his lord, moved with anger, handed him over to the torturers until he should repay all that was owed him."

"Well," you say, "that was just a parable. We can't press every point and say each little detail applies to us." Granted, but in this case, it's not a *little* detail. It is the punch line, the climax of the whole story. How can I say that? Because verse 35 is not part of the parable. It is a statement Jesus makes *after* the story ends. It is His penetrating application of the whole parable on forgiving others.

He wrapped up His instruction with this grim warning: "So shall My heavenly Father also do to you, if each of you does not forgive his brother from your heart."

Candidly, this is one of the most important truths God ever revealed to me on the consequences of an unforgiving spirit. When Jesus says, "So shall My heavenly Father also do to you . . . ," He is referring back to the closing words of the parable:

"And his lord, moved with anger, handed

*him over to the torturers until he should
repay all that was owed him."*

This is no fictitious tale, like Bluebeard
who tortured others behind a secret door. No,
Jesus says God personally will allow those who
refuse to forgive others to be tortured.

What in the world does that mean? The
root Greek term from which "torturers" is
translated is a verb meaning "to torment"—a
frightening thought. When I first saw the
thing begin to take shape in my mind, I re-
sisted it. I thought, No, that's too harsh! But
the further I probed, the clearer it became.

The same term is used to describe a person suffering "great pain" (Matt. 8:6). It is
also used to describe the misery of a man being
"in agony" in hell as he pleads for relief (Luke
16:23–24). When we read of a man named
Lot, in 2 Peter 2:8, who was surrounded and
oppressed by the conduct of unprincipled
men, we read "his righteous soul [was] tor-
mented day after day." Again the same Greek
term is used. Pain, agony, and torment are all
a part of this torturous experience.

But here in Matthew 18:34–35, Jesus re-
fers to *torturers*—a noun, not a verb. He is
saying the one who refuses to forgive, the
Christian who harbors grudges and entertains
bitter feelings toward another, will be turned
over to torturous thoughts, feelings of misery,
and agonizing unrest within. One fine exposi-
tor describes it like this:

This is a marvelously expressive phrase to describe what happens to us when we do not forgive another. It is an accurate description of gnawing resentment and bitterness, the awful gall of hate or envy. It is a terrible feeling. We cannot get away from it, we cannot escape it. We find ourselves powerless to avoid it. We feel strongly this separation from another and every time we think of them we feel within the acid of resentment and hate eating away at our peace and calmness. This is the torturing that our Lord says will take place.[5]

And who hasn't endured such feelings? I certainly have! It is one of the horrible consequences of *not* forgiving those who offend us. It makes no difference who it is—one of your parents or in-laws, your pastor or former pastor, a close friend who turned against you, some teacher who was unfair, or a business partner who ripped you off . . . even your former mate in marriage. I meet many divorced people who have been "handed over to the torturers" for this very reason. Believe me, it is not worth the misery. The solution? Forgive as we have been forgiven! Release the poison of all that bitterness . . . let it gush out before God, and declare your sincere desire to be free. It's one of the essential steps each of us must take toward becoming a genuine Christian in the eyes of the world.

Perhaps it would be helpful for me to clarify how this applies when we have been victimized through abuse, rape, assault, incest, or some other heinous crime. God has originated governments to maintain and carry out laws in a civilized culture. It is not unchristian to use those laws for personal protection and to seek civil justice. As I said at the beginning, criminal acts need to be punished and torturous abuses must be brought before the courts. I find nothing in Scripture that encourages the silent endurance of physical and emotional harm. But what is important for our own mental health and emotional stability is the forgiveness of those who wrong us . . . "seventy times seven." It has been my observation that the courtroom—as essential and effective as it may be—is not a place that nurtures the spirit of forgiveness. That must come from the heart. If the heart is saturated with anger, hatred, and bitterness, we become victims of our own venom, which results in our being "handed over to the torturers," as Jesus put it.

HOW TO MAKE IT HAPPEN

There is enough in the preceding pages to keep us thinking—and forgiving—for weeks. But there are a couple specifics that need to be considered before we proceed to the flip side of this vital issue.

First, *focus fully on God's forgiveness of*

you. Don't hurry through this. Think of how vast, how extensive is His mercy which has been extended toward you. Like Aaron, the young seminary student, must have done in the courtroom that day. Like David did when he wrote "Hymn 103." He got extremely specific. Remember?

> *Bless the Lord, O my soul,*
> *And forget none of His benefits;*
> *Who pardons all your iniquities;*
> *Who heals all your diseases;*
> *Who redeems your life from the pit;*
> *Who crowns you with lovingkindness*
> *   and compassion;*
> *Who satisfies your years with good*
> *   things,*
> *So that your youth is renewed like the*
> *   eagle. . . .*
> *He has not dealt with us according to*
> *   our sins,*
> *Nor rewarded us according to our*
> *   iniquities.*
> *For as high as the heavens are above*
> *   the earth,*
> *So great is His lovingkindness toward*
> *   those who fear Him.*
> *As far as the east is from the west,*
> *So far has He removed our transgres-*
> *   sions from us.*
> *(Ps. 103:2–5, 10–12)*

Meditate on that in your own life. Personalize the words by substituting *me* and *my* for *us* and *your.* Ponder the depth of God's mercy . . . the debts against you He graciously canceled. The extent to which you can envision God's forgiveness of you, to that same measure you will be given the capacity to forgive others. As you allow this to happen, relief and freedom will release you from the paralysis of your own poison.

Next, *deal directly and honestly with any resentment you currently hold against anyone.*

It's a tough exam, I repeat. But think of the alternative—torturing, agonizing feelings, the churning within, the enormous emotional energy you burn up and waste every day.

Maybe you are willing to go just so far. You will bargain with God and agree to forgive *but not forget.* That is one of the most regrettable mistakes a servant-in-the-making can make. Why? Because limited forgiveness is like conditional love—a poor substitute for the genuine item. It really amounts to no forgiveness at all.

Amy Carmichael said it best when she wrote these words:

> *If I say, "Yes, I forgive, but I cannot forget," as though the God, who twice a day washes all the sands on all the shores of all the world, could not wash such memories from my mind, then I know nothing of Calvary love.*[6]

My prayer for you is that God will soften the soil of your soul so completely that you will be able to do whatever is necessary to make forgiveness a reality. Perhaps it will help if you commit the following words to memory. They have come to my rescue numerous times:

> *We are most like beasts when we kill.*
> *We are most like men when we judge.*
> *We are most like God when we forgive.*[7]

His heart was as great as the world, but there was no room in it to hold the memory of a wrong.—*Emerson*

FORGETTING

'll forgive . . . but I'll never forget." We say and hear this so much that it's easy to shrug it off and think, "Well, it's only natural." Unfortunately, therein lies the problem. It is the most natural response we can expect. Not *super*natural. It also can result in tragic consequences.

Several years ago I read of two unmarried sisters who lived together, but because of an unresolved disagreement, they stopped speaking to each other (one of the many inescapable results of refusing to forgive and forget). Since they were either unable or unwilling to move out of their small house, they continued to exist in the same dwelling, eat at the same table, use the same appliances, and sleep in the same room . . . all separately . . . without saying one word. A chalk line divided the sleeping area into two halves, separating the doorway as well as the fireplace. Each would come and go, cook and eat, sew and read without ever stepping over into her sister's territory. Through the black of the night, each could hear the deep breathing of the other, but because both were unwilling to take the first step toward forgiving and forgetting the long-standing offense, they coexisted *for years* in grinding silence.[1]

Refusing to forgive *and forget* leads to other tragedies, like monuments of spite. How many churches split (often over nit-picking issues), then spin off into another direction—fractured, splintered, angry, and blindly opinionated?

After I spoke at a summer Bible conference meeting one evening, a lady told me she and her family had been camping across America. In their travels they drove through a town and passed a church with a name she said she would never forget—THE ORIGINAL CHURCH OF GOD, NUMBER TWO.

Whether a personal or public matter, we quickly reveal whether we possess a servant's heart in how we respond to those who have offended us. And it isn't enough simply to say, "Well, OK—you're forgiven, but don't expect me to forget it!" That means we have erected a monument of spite in our mind, which could hardly be considered forgiveness. Christians must be big people. Big enough to *go on,* remembering the right and forgetting the wrong. Like the age-old saying, "Write injuries in dust, benefits in marble."[2]

CAN THE MIND EVER FORGET?

A number of years ago I met a very fine young woman who was married to a physician. One day her husband told her that he had "fallen out of love with her." At the time they had two sons. From that day on, life just got worse. He abused, ignored, maligned, embarrassed, and hurt her. While she was pregnant with their third child, he walked out and ultimately divorced her.

She remembered driving her car to the

hospital to deliver their child—alone, no one there, no one caring, no one listening, no one noticing. Except Christ Jesus, who saw her through the birth, and then began to wash her mind of those painful memories.

It so happened that her path crossed with that of a young man whom she had known in high school. They had been sweethearts, in fact. He, too, was a doctor now. He had never married. Well, they fell in love and were soon married. That was years ago, but when I ran into this woman a while back, I asked her how her life was now in comparison to the way it had been. All she said was, "Chuck, I don't even remember how things were." What a beautiful illustration of the mercy and grace of God.

But a question flashes through my head as I write these words: Can our minds actually *allow* us to forget? The way God has made us—with that internal filing system we call *memory*—it is doubtful that we can fully forget even the things we *want* to forget.

Our minds are simply remarkable. My longtime friend, Dr. Earl Radmacher, aptly illustrates the truth of that statement.

> *The human mind is a fabulous computer. As a matter of fact, no one has been able to design a computer as intricate and efficient as the human mind. Consider this: your brain is capable of recording 800 memories per*

second for seventy-five years without ever getting tired. . . .

I have heard some persons complain that their brain is too tired to get involved in a program of Scripture memorization. I have news for them— the body can get tired, but the brain never does. A human being doesn't use more than 2 percent of his brain power, scientists tell us. And, of course, some demonstrate this fact more obviously than others. The point is, the brain is capable of an incredible amount of work and it retains everything it takes in. You never really forget anything; you just don't recall it. Everything is on permanent file in your brain.[3]

Because of facts like these, you need to understand that I'm not referring to forgetting in the technical or literal sense of the term. Rather, I'm thinking about forgetting the same way Paul does in 1 Corinthians 13:4–5 when he says:

Love is patient, love is kind, and is not jealous; love does not brag and is not arrogant, does not act unbecomingly; it does not seek its own, is not provoked, does not take into account a wrong suffered.

That statement is rendered this way in the J. B. Phillips New Testament:

> *This love of which I speak is slow to lose patience—it looks for a way of being constructive. It is not possessive: it is neither anxious to impress nor does it cherish inflated ideas of its own importance.*
>
> *Love has good manners and does not pursue selfish advantage. It is not touchy. It does not keep account of evil or gloat over the wickedness of other people. On the contrary, it shares the joy of those who live by the truth.*[4]

True believers, when demonstrating genuine love, don't harbor their hurts. Webster defines *forget* as "to lose the remembrance of . . . to treat with inattention or disregard . . . to disregard intentionally: OVERLOOK . . . to cease remembering or noticing . . . to fail to become mindful at the proper time."[5] That's the thought.

A couple of Scriptures illustrate and encourage this greathearted virtue.

> *Those who love Thy law have great peace,*
> *And nothing causes them to stumble.*
> *(Ps. 119:165)*

The psalmist declares that those who possess a deep love for God's Word possess great measures of His *shalom* . . . and, in addition, they will be big enough to resist stumbling over offenses, either petty or pronounced.

Jesus hinted at this when He spoke out against a judgmental spirit. Read His words carefully.

"Do not judge lest you be judged yourselves. For in the way you judge, you will be judged; and by your standard of measure, it will be measured to you. And why do you look at the speck that is in your brother's eye, but do not notice the log that is in your own eye? Or how can you say to your brother, 'Let me take the speck out of your eye,' and behold, the log is in your own eye? You hypocrite, first take the log out of your own eye, and then you will see clearly to take the speck out of your brother's eye." (Matt. 7:1–5)

So then, as we talk about *forgetting*, let's understand that we mean:

- Refusing to keep score (1 Cor. 13:5).
- Being bigger than any offense (Ps. 119:165).
- Harboring no judgmental attitudes (Matt. 7:1–5).

Remember the true story of the man I mentioned at the beginning of this minibook . . . the seminary student who deliberately overlooked the offenses of those thugs? When you analyze his response, you realize he exemplified all three of those characteristics.

Before proceeding, I'd like to clarify

something. I have in mind the ability to go on beyond our own good deeds. Once they are done, they're done. No need to drop little hints on how thoughtful we were. How pleasant it is to meet a few folks in life who don't call attention to all the great things they do for others!

A CLOSE LOOK AT FORGETTING

Tucked away in the New Testament is a chapter that illustrates this truth beautifully. It's Philippians, chapter 3. The writer, Paul, is listing a number of things in his past that could easily feed his pride.

> *If anyone else has a mind to put confidence in the flesh, I far more: circumcised the eighth day, of the nation of Israel, of the tribe of Benjamin, a Hebrew of Hebrews; as to the Law, a Pharisee; as to zeal, a persecutor of the church; as to the righteousness which is in the Law, found blameless. (vv. 4b–6)*

If you were looking for somebody to give a testimony next Sunday, Paul would be a winner. (If he let himself, he could easily turn it into a "braggimony.") These are impressive facts . . . and they are absolutely true.

But Paul, humble servant of Christ that he was, kept it all in proper perspective.

> *But whatever things were gain to me, those things I have counted as loss for*

> *the sake of Christ. More than that, I count all things to be loss in view of the surpassing value of knowing Christ Jesus my Lord, for whom I have suffered the loss of all things, and count them but rubbish in order that I may gain Christ. (vv. 7–9)*

In comparison to Jesus Christ and all the things He has made possible—His forgiveness, His love, His righteousness—everything else we may be or may do diminishes in significance. Paul's following words describe the healthy humility of a follower of Christ:

> *I don't mean to say I am perfect. I haven't learned all I should even yet, but I keep working toward that day when I will finally be all that Christ saved me for and wants me to be.*
>
> *No, dear brothers, I am still not all I should be but I am bringing all my energies to bear on this one thing: Forgetting the past and looking forward to what lies ahead, I strain to reach the end of the race and receive the prize for which God is calling us up to heaven because of what Christ Jesus did for us. (vv. 12–14)[6]*

Woven into these words are three implications: (1) "I have not arrived," (2) "I forget what is behind," and (3) "I move on to what is ahead."

Within each of these, I find an important characteristic of Christlike servanthood: vulnerability, humility, and determination.

Vulnerability

"I have not arrived" is a concept that Paul mentions no less than three times in Philippians 2:12–13:

1. "Not that I have already obtained it" (v. 12).
2. "Or have already become perfect" (v. 12).
3. "I do not regard myself as having laid hold of it yet" (v. 13).

How refreshing!

Here is this brilliant, competent, gifted, strong leader who freely declares, "I don't have everything in life wired." Vulnerability includes more than this, however. It means being willing to express personal needs, admitting one's own limitations or failures, having a teachable spirit, and *especially* being reluctant to appear the expert, an apostolic know-it-all, the final voice of authority. Not only are these traits refreshing, they're rare!

If you're the type of person who always has to come out right . . . if you have the need to appear "perfect," then you will always be in the position of having something to prove. And the others around you will feel the need to do the same.

Executive Howard Butt, a businessman

in Corpus Christi, Texas, writes of this in a very honest and practical manner.

If your leadership is Christian you can openly reveal your failures. Leaders who are fully human do not hide their sins. Within you operates the principle of the cross, the modus operandi of strength in weakness.

This principle points up our problem—we who are religious. We want a Christian reputation more than we want Christ. And yet our Lord, becoming sin for us, "made himself of no reputation." . . .

Am I willing to hide my strengths and reveal my weaknesses? Are you? Telling our triumphs, our successes, our achievements, we glorify ourselves. . . . Bragging about my goodness, I build barriers up; when I confess my sins, those barriers come down. Pagan outsiders get driven away by our pious parade of religious achievements. Building our high walls of intimidation, we make their friendly corner bartender look good. Christians are not half-angels with high-beam halos, but real live forgiven sinners up close. . . .

Christ's death frees you from hiding your sins. You can be vulnerable and open. When you are weak then you are strong. You shake the darkness with irresistible blows: the divine might

of weakness. You hit your hardest when
your guard is down.[7]

Being vulnerable is part of being a person
who forgets.

Humility

"I forget what is behind" is a statement
that assures us Paul was not the type to live
in the past. He says, in effect, "I disregard
my own accomplishments as well as others'
offenses against me. I refuse to dwell on that."
This requires humility. Especially when you
examine Paul's past. His litany of painful
achievements is mind-boggling.

> *Five times I received from the Jews
> thirty-nine lashes. Three times I was
> beaten with rods, once I was stoned,
> three times I was shipwrecked, a night
> and a day I have spent in the deep.
> I have been on frequent journeys, in
> dangers from rivers, dangers from rob-
> bers, dangers from my countrymen,
> dangers from the Gentiles, dangers in
> the city, dangers in the wilderness,
> dangers on the sea, dangers among the
> false brethren; I have been in labor and
> hardship, through many sleepless nights,
> in hunger and thirst, often without
> food, in cold and exposure.*
> *(2 Cor. 11:24–27)*

Think of all the people Paul could have
included on his "hate list." But he had no

such list. Nobody's face was on Paul's mental dart board. With humility, he forgot what was behind him. He intentionally disregarded all those wrongs against him.

The very best example of forgetting that I can think of is a remarkable man named Joseph in the book of Genesis. Rejected and hated by his brothers, sold to a group of travelers in a caravan destined for Egypt, sold again as a common slave in the Egyptian market, falsely accused by Potiphar's wife, forgotten in a dungeon, and considered dead by his own father, this man was finally promoted to a position of high authority just beneath the pharaoh. If anybody ever had a reason to lick his wounds and despise his past, Joseph was the man!

But the amazing part of the story is this: he refused to remember the offenses. In fact, when he and his wife had their first child, he named the boy Manasseh, a Hebrew word that means "forget." He explains the reason he chose the name:

> *And Joseph named the first-born Manasseh, "For," he said, "God has made me forget all my trouble and all my father's household." (Gen. 41:51)*

His words include an extremely important point. In order for us to forget wrongs done against us, *God* must be allowed to do the erasing.

Isaiah, the prophet of Judah, puts it in these terms:

> *"Fear not, for you will not be put to shame;*
> *Neither feel humiliated, for you will not be disgraced;*
> *But you will forget the shame of your youth,*
> *And the reproach of your widowhood you will remember no more.*
> *For your husband is your Maker,*
> *Whose name is the Lord of hosts;*
> *And your Redeemer is the Holy One of Israel,*
> *Who is called the God of all the earth."*
> (Isa. 54:4–5)

The Lord God promises us we can forget because He personally will fill the void of those painful memories. To you who have had a shameful youth, to you who have lost your mate, to you who have been overlooked, despised, rejected, and mistreated, the living Lord will replace those awful memories *with Himself.* Great promise! That makes the forgetting possible. Left to ourselves, no way! But with the promise that God will replace the pain with Himself—His presence, His power, His very life—we can forget what lies behind.

There is yet another characteristic of true Christianity in addition to vulnerability and humility. It's implied in the words "I press on toward the goal" (Phil. 3:14).

Determination

Those who refuse to get bogged down in and anchored to the past are those who pursue the objectives of the future. Such people are not petty. They are too involved in getting today's job done to be occupied with yesterday's hurts and concerns. Very near the end of his full and productive life, Paul wrote: "I have fought the good fight, I have finished the course, I have kept the faith" (2 Tim. 4:7). What a grand epitaph! He seized every day by the throat. He relentlessly pursued life.

I know human nature well enough to realize that some people excuse their bitterness over past hurts by thinking, "It's too late to change. I've been injured and the wrong done against me is too great ever to forget. Maybe Paul could press on—but not me!" People with this mind-set are convinced that they are the exception to the truths of Scripture, and they are determined not to change because "life has dealt them a bad hand."

But when God holds out hope, when God makes promises, when God says, "It can be done," there are *no exceptions.* With each new dawn there is delivered to your door a fresh, new package called "today." God has designed us in such a way that we can handle only one package at a time . . . and all the grace we need will be supplied by Him as we live out that day.

I cannot recall a more moving illustration of this truth than the true story my friend

John Haggai tells regarding the tragic birth and life of his son. I share it with you in detail with the hope that at least one person will discover the all-important secret of pressing on only one day at a time.

The Lord graciously blessed us with a precious son. He was paralyzed and able to sit in his wheelchair only with the assistance of full-length body braces. One of the nation's most respected gynecologists and obstetricians brought him into the world. Tragically, this man—overcome by grief—sought to find the answer in a bourbon bottle rather than in the blessed Bible. Due to the doctor's intoxication at the time of delivery, he inexcusably bungled his responsibility. Several of the baby's bones were broken. His leg was pulled out at the growing center. Needless abuse—resulting in hemorrhaging of the brain—was inflicted upon the little fellow. (Let me pause long enough to say that this is no indictment upon doctors. I thank God for doctors. This man was a tragic exception. He was banned from practice in some hospitals, and [later] he committed suicide.)

During the first year of the little lad's life, eight doctors said he could not possibly survive. For the first two years of his life my wife had to feed him every three hours with a Brecht feeder. It took a half hour to prepare for the feeding and it took another half hour to clean up and put him back to bed. Not once during that time did she get out of the house for any diversion whatsoever. Never did she get more than two hours sleep at one time.

My wife, formerly Christine Barker of Bristol, Virginia, had once been acclaimed by some of the nation's leading musicians as one of the outstanding contemporary female vocalists in America. From the time she was 13 she had been popular as a singer—and constantly in the public eye. Hers was the experience of receiving and rejecting some fancy offers with even fancier incomes to marry an aspiring Baptist pastor with no church to pastor!

Then, after five years of marriage, tragedy struck! The whole episode was so unnecessary. From a life of public service she was now marooned within the walls of our home. Her beautiful voice no longer enraptured public audiences with the story of Jesus, but was now silenced, or at best, muted to the subdued humming of lullabies.

Had it not been for her spiritual maturity whereby she laid hold of the resources of God and lived one day at a time, this heart-rending experience *would long since have caused an emotional breakdown.*

John Edmund, Jr., our little son, lived 24 years and died in 1975. We rejoice that he committed his heart and life to Jesus Christ and gave evidence of a genuine concern for the things of the Lord. I attribute his commitment to Jesus Christ and his wonderful disposition to the sparkling radiance of an emotionally mature, Christ-centered mother who has mastered the discipline of living one day at a time. Never have I—nor has anyone else—heard a word of complaint from her. The people who know her concur that . . . after having been subjected to more grief than many people twice her age, she possessed sparkle that would be the envy of any high school senior and the radiance and charm for which any debutante would gladly give a fortune.

Seize today. Live for today. Wring it dry of every opportunity.[8]

A CHALLENGE: TWO QUESTIONS

Forgiving is essential. It is also usually rewarded with relief and encouragement that follow on the heels of our forgiving another. But forgetting is something shared with no other person. It's a solo flight. And all the rewards are postponed until eternity . . . but how great they will be on that day! Forgetting requires us to think correctly, which means our full focus must be on the Lord and not on humanity. By God's great grace, it can happen.

As I bring my thoughts to a close, let's pause long enough to ask ourselves two questions.

First: Is there someone or something I have refused to forgive and/or forget, which keeps me from living a happy, free, and productive life?

If your answer is yes, stop and declare it openly to your Lord, asking Him to take away the pain and the bitterness. Go to whatever lengths necessary to rid yourself of this enormous burden.

Second: Am I a victim of self-pity, living out my days emotionally paralyzed in anguish and despair?

If your answer is yes, stop and consider the consequences of living the rest of your life excusing your depression rather than turning it all over to the only One who can help you through it.

And lest you are still convinced it's "too late" . . . you are "too old to change" . . . your situation is "too much to overcome," consider the immortal lines of Longfellow.

> It is too late! Ah, nothing is too late
> Till the tired heart shall cease to palpitate.
> Cato learned Greek at eighty; Sophocles

Wrote his grand Oedipus, and Simonides
Bore off the prize of verse from his
    compeers,
When each had numbered more than
    fourscore years,
And Theophrastus, at fourscore and
    ten,
Had but begun his "Characters of Men."
Chaucer, at Woodstock with the night-
    ingales,
At sixty wrote the Canterbury Tales;
Goethe at Weimar, toiling to the last,
Completed Faust when eighty years
    were past. . . .
What then? Shall we sit idly down and
    say
The night hath come; it is no longer
    day? . . .
For age is opportunity no less
Than youth itself, though in another
    dress,
And as the evening twilight fades away
The sky is filled with stars, invisible by
    day.[9]

It is never too late to start doing what is right. Forgive, my friend . . . and forget! By doing so you will enter into a freedom you've never dreamed possible.

Dear forgiving Father,

Thank You so much for Your mercy . . . for accepting us as we are and for releasing us from the bondage of our sin. I am so grateful that You are a forgiving God. Make us like You are, Lord. Give us the courage to face the truth, which ultimately sets us free. Where we have caused an offense, make us quick to acknowledge our wrong and then do whatever is necessary to be reconciled to the people we have offended. And with those who have hurt or wronged us, may we release all resentment and refuse to hold a grudge. Keep us free of those awful torturers, Lord! And as You free us, enable us to forget whatever those things are that hold us back, causing us to live counterproductive lives.

Finally, may we come to the place where we find our greatest joy in granting others what they do not deserve . . . and thereby set the prisoners free from bondage, namely ourselves.

In the grace of Your Son,
Amen

NOTES

Forgiving

1. Horatio G. Spafford, "It Is Well with My Soul," in *The Hymnal for Worship and Celebration* (Waco, Tex.: Word Music, 1986), no. 493.

2. G. Abbott-Smith, *A Manual Greek Lexicon of the New Testament,* 3d ed. (Edinburgh, Scotland: T. and T. Clark, 1937), p. 109.

3. Gerhard Kittel, ed., *Theological Dictionary of the New Testament,* trans. and ed. Geoffrey W. Bromiley (Grand Rapids, Mich.: William B. Eerdmans Publishing Co., 1964), vol. 1, p. 253.

4. Charles H. Gabriel, "My Evening Prayer," in *The Best Loved Poems of the American People,* selected by Hazel Felleman (Garden City, N.Y.: Garden City Publishing, 1936), p. 297.

5. Ray C. Stedman, "Breaking the Resentment Barrier," Treasures of the Parables Series (Palo Alto, Calif.: Discovery Publishing, n.d.), message 11.

6. Amy Carmichael, *If,* ©1938 Dohnavur Fellowship (Fort Washington, Pa.: Christian Literature Crusade). Used by permission. All rights reserved.

7. William Arthur Ward, *Thoughts of a Christian Optimist* (Anderson, S.C.: Droke House, Publishers, 1968), p. 48.

Forgetting

1. Leslie B. Flynn, *When the Saints Come Storming In,* updated and expanded (Wheaton, Ill.: SP Publications, Victor Books, 1988), p. 143. This book was formerly titled *Great Church Fights.*

2. Benjamin Franklin, as quoted by Flynn in *When the Saints Come Storming In,* p. 91.

3. Earl D. Radmacher, *You and Your Thoughts: The Power of Right Thinking* (Wheaton, Ill.: Tyndale House Publishers, 1977), pp. 15, 19.

4. J. B. Phillips, The New Testament in Modern English, rev. ed. (New York, N.Y.: Macmillan Publishing Co., 1972).

5. *Webster's Ninth New Collegiate Dictionary,* see "forget."

6. The Living Bible (Wheaton, Ill.: Tyndale House Publishers, 1971).

7. Howard Butt, *The Velvet Covered Brick: Christian Leadership in an Age of Rebellion* (New York, N.Y.: Harper and Row, Publishers, 1973), pp. 41–43.

8. John Haggai, *How to Win Over Worry* (Eugene, Oreg.: Harvest House Publishers, 1987), pp. 110–11.

9. Henry Wadsworth Longfellow, excerpt from *Morituri Salutamus,* from *The Poetical Works of Longfellow* (Boston, Mass.: Houghton Mifflin Co., 1975), pp. 313–14.

MY DIARY OF FORGIVENESS

Personal Thoughts and Discoveries
about Forgiving and Forgetting